INSIDE THE NFL

Kansas City Chiefs

BY ZACH WYNER

www.av2books.com

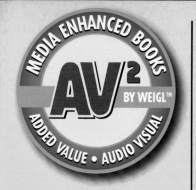

AV² provides enriched content that supplements and complements this book. Weigl's AV² books strive to create inspired learning and engage young minds in a total learning experience.

Your AV² Media Enhanced books come alive with...

Audio
Listen to sections of the book read aloud.

Key Words
Study vocabulary, and complete a matching word activity.

Go to **www.av2books.com**, and enter this book's unique code.

Video
Watch informative video clips.

Quizzes
Test your knowledge.

BOOK CODE

W476678

Embedded Weblinks
Gain additional information for research.

Slide Show
View images and captions, and prepare a presentation.

AV² by Weigl brings you media enhanced books that support active learning.

Try This!
Complete activities and hands-on experiments.

... and much, much more!

Published by AV² by Weigl
350 5th Avenue, 59th Floor
New York, NY 10118
Websites: www.av2books.com   www.weigl.com

Library of Congress Control Number: 2014930849

ISBN 978-1-4896-0842-0 (hardcover)
ISBN 978-1-4896-0844-4 (single user ebook)
ISBN 978-1-4896-0845-1 (multi user ebook)

Printed in the United States of America in Brainerd, Minnesota
3 4 5 6 7 8 9 0   20 19 18 17 16

022016
290216

Project Coordinator Aaron Carr
Art Director Terry Paulhus

Photo Credits
Every reasonable effort has been made to trace ownership and to obtain permission to reprint copyright material. The publishers would be pleased to have any errors or omissions brought to their attention so that they may be corrected in subsequent printings.

Weigl acknowledges Getty Images as its primary image supplier for this title.

Kansas City Chiefs

CONTENTS

Introduction

A team with a long and storied history, the Kansas City Chiefs have a dedicated fan base and are at the heart of some of the league's most historic rivalries. They are the owners of three American Football League (AFL) titles and their victory in **Super Bowl** IV helped bring about a **merger** between the AFL and the National Football League (NFL).

Following a tough 2012 season, Head Coach Andy Reid has led a comeback in Kansas City. In 2013, the Chiefs placed among the NFL's top six teams in both offense and defense. They transformed from a 2-14 win-loss record the year before to an 11-5 record and a trip to the playoffs.

The Chiefs enjoyed a nine-win improvement from 2012 to 2013.

With multiple **Pro Bowlers** on both sides of the ball, the Kansas City Chiefs are interested in more than qualifying for the **postseason**. The Chiefs seek their first Super Bowl appearance since 1970.

Jamaal Charles is the current starting running back of the Chiefs. He was drafted by Kansas City in 2008.

Stadium Arrowhead Stadium

Division American Football Conference (AFC) West

Head coach Andy Reid

Location Kansas City, Missouri

NFL championships 1969

Nicknames Arrowheads

17 Playoff Appearances

1 NFL Championship

8 Division Championships

History

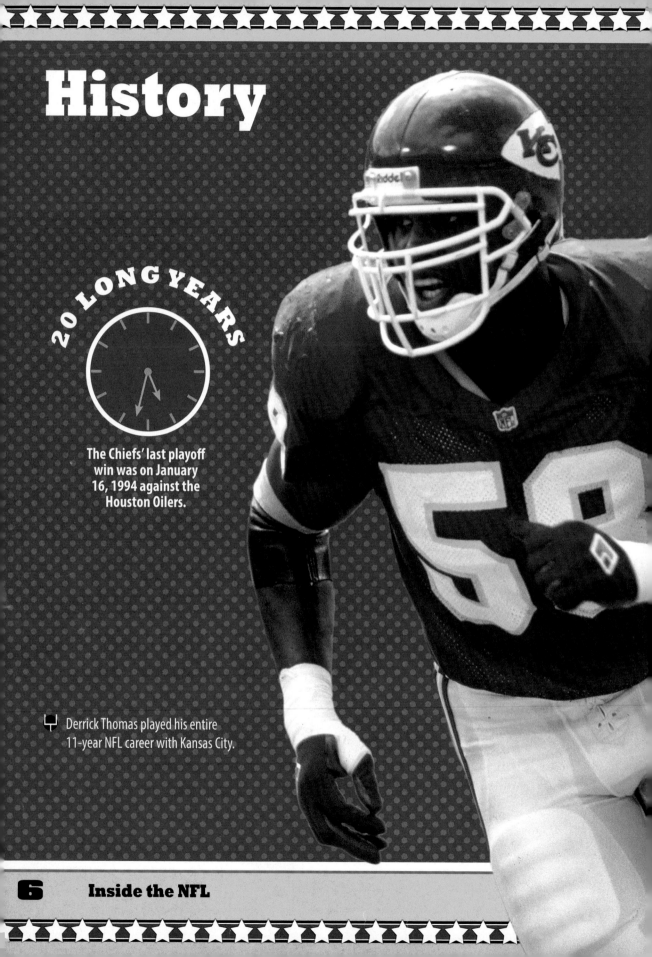

20 LONG YEARS

The Chiefs' last playoff win was on January 16, 1994 against the Houston Oilers.

Derrick Thomas played his entire 11-year NFL career with Kansas City.

n 1960, Lamar Hunt's Dallas Texans were one of eight **inaugural** AFL teams. Two years later, head coach Hank Stram led the Texans to the AFL Championship. When it became clear that the city of Dallas could not support two professional football teams, Hunt moved his AFL-Champion Texans to Kansas City.

Renamed the "Chiefs," Hunt's team quickly created a new identity for themselves in the Midwest. Led by Len Dawson, Otis Taylor, Bobby Bell, Johnny Robinson, and Buck Buchanan, the Chiefs captured the 1966 AFL title. In 1969, the Chiefs won a third AFL Championship. Then, they shocked the NFL champion Minnesota Vikings in Super Bowl IV, winning by a score of 23-7.

After a 14-year playoff drought, the Chiefs started winning again under head coach Marty Schottenheimer and **hall of fame** linebacker Derrick Thomas. Thomas and teammate Neil Smith were a huge threat to offenses. Former Los Angeles running back Marcus Allen signed with the Chiefs in 1993 and sparked the team to their first division title in more than 20 years. Pro Bowlers Tony Gonzalez, Priest Holmes, Dante Hall, Trent Green, and Jamaal Charles helped the Chiefs win two division titles in the 2000s. However, the Chiefs have not won a playoff game since the 1993 season. With the hiring of Andy Reid in 2013, Kansas City is sure that streak will soon come to an end.

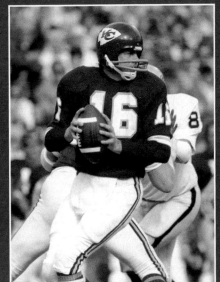

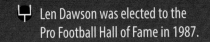 Len Dawson was elected to the Pro Football Hall of Fame in 1987.

The Stadium

Arrowhead Stadium seats 79,451 fans.

The Kansas City Chiefs have one of the longest residencies in the NFL. In addition, the faithful fans that pack Arrowhead Stadium for every Chiefs home game can brag about one of the loudest environments in the NFL. In October of 2013, Chiefs fans entered the Guinness World Records by setting an NFL record with a cheer that measured 137.5 decibels.

A jet engine can reach a sound level of 140 decibels, which is just about the same noise level as a Kansas City crowd.

Being an older stadium, Arrowhead has required some renovations over the years. The most recent began in 2007 and were completed in 2010. During that time, new high definition video screens were installed along with more luxury seating and a Chiefs Hall of Honor that pays tribute to Kansas City's best players.

For nearly 50 years, from 1960 to 2008, Arrowhead Stadium was lucky enough to be home to the TD Pack Band. Led by trumpeter Tony DiPardo, the TD Pack Band was famous for writing songs such as "The Chiefs are on the Warpath" and "The Hank Stram Polka." An integral part of the Chiefs' family, the Chiefs awarded DiPardo a Super Bowl ring after their victory in Super Bowl IV.

Hungry Chiefs fans flock to Gates BBQ for giant beef sandwiches and fries.

W**■■■** T**■■**y Pl**■**y

CANADA

30 Washington

Oregon

Montana

North Dakota

Minnesota

Lake Superior

Idaho

23 Wisconsin

22

29

15

Nevada

Utah

Wyoming

South Dakota

Nebraska

Iowa

24

13 Illinois

California

Colorado

14

Kansas

Missouri

31

UNITED STATES

16

Arizona

New Mexico

Oklahoma

Arkansas

Pacific Ocean

32

Texas

17

Mississippi

12

Louisiana

27

Alaska

Hawaiʻi

MEXICO

Gulf of Mexico

0   500 Miles
0   500 km

0   100 Miles
0   100 km

A

AMERICAN FOOTBALL CONFERENCE

EAST		NORTH		SOUTH		WEST	
1	Gillette Stadium	5	FirstEnergy Stadium	9	EverBank Field	★ 13	Arrowhead Stadium
2	MetLife Stadium	6	Heinz Field	10	LP Field	14	Sports Authority Field at Mile High
3	Ralph Wilson Stadium	7	M&T Bank Stadium	11	Lucas Oil Stadium	15	O.co Coliseum
4	Sun Life Stadium	8	Paul Brown Stadium	12	NRG Stadium	16	Qualcomm Stadium

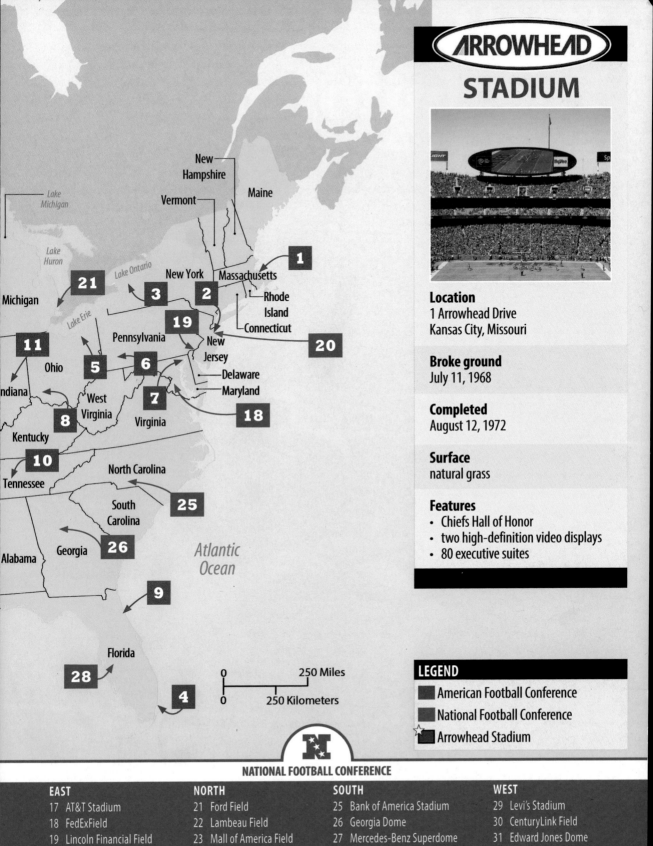

ARROWHEAD STADIUM

Location
1 Arrowhead Drive
Kansas City, Missouri

Broke ground
July 11, 1968

Completed
August 12, 1972

Surface
natural grass

Features
- Chiefs Hall of Honor
- two high-definition video displays
- 80 executive suites

LEGEND
- American Football Conference
- National Football Conference
- ☆ Arrowhead Stadium

Lake Michigan

Lake Huron

Lake Ontario

Lake Erie

Michigan

New Hampshire

Maine

Vermont

New York

Massachusetts

Rhode Island

Connecticut

1

21

3

2

19

20

11

Pennsylvania

New Jersey

5

6

Delaware

Ohio

Maryland

Indiana

West Virginia

7

18

8

Virginia

Kentucky

10

North Carolina

Tennessee

25

South Carolina

26

Atlantic Ocean

Alabama

Georgia

9

Florida

28

4

| 0 | 250 Miles |
| 0 | 250 Kilometers |

N

NATIONAL FOOTBALL CONFERENCE

EAST	NORTH	SOUTH	WEST
17 AT&T Stadium	21 Ford Field	25 Bank of America Stadium	29 Levi's Stadium
18 FedExField	22 Lambeau Field	26 Georgia Dome	30 CenturyLink Field
19 Lincoln Financial Field	23 Mall of America Field	27 Mercedes-Benz Superdome	31 Edward Jones Dome
20 MetLife Stadium	24 Soldier Field	28 Raymond James Stadium	32 University of Phoenix Stadium

The Uniforms

RED ON RED

01

The Chiefs wore their red jerseys with red pants for the first time in team history for the 2013 home opener.

As starting quarterback for the Chiefs, Alex Smith helped guide Kansas City to an 11–5 record during the 2013 regular season.

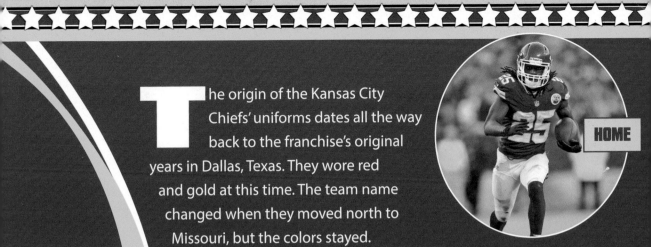

The origin of the Kansas City Chiefs' uniforms dates all the way back to the franchise's original years in Dallas, Texas. They wore red and gold at this time. The team name changed when they moved north to Missouri, but the colors stayed.

HOME

Over the years, the Chiefs have made only minor alterations to their original uniform. The uniform has either a red jersey with white pants and white numbers or a white jersey with white numbers and red pants. Gold and red stripes appear on both the pants and the jersey sleeves. At times, Chiefs have worn all-white uniforms on the road. Since Lamar Hunt's death in 2006, the team has sometimes worn these jerseys in honor of their former owner.

AWAY

The Chiefs' jerseys pay tribute to Lamar Hunt, with the initials "LH" permanently attached to the left chest of every uniform.

The Helmets

TO THE LETTER

The Chiefs are one of only four teams to wear their city's **INITIALS** on their helmet. The other teams are the New York Giants, San Francisco 49ers, and Baltimore Ravens.

The Chiefs copied the San Francisco 49ers in the way the 49ers merged the "SF" on their helmets when they locked the "KC" together on theirs.

From the Chiefs' beginning in 1963 until today, the interlocking letters "KC" have decorated either side of the red Chiefs' helmet. They appear inside an arrowhead with the intention of recalling the American Indians that once populated the state of Missouri. The **logo** also pays tribute to the Tribe of Mic-O-Say, a branch of the Boy Scouts of America. Founded by former Kansas City mayor H. Roe Bartle, this group taught the values and ideals of the Arapaho American Indians.

The Chiefs' helmet design is both simple and iconic. It looks like the American Indian arrowhead. This tool was once used by American Indians to hunt for food. It also functioned as a weapon used in defense of their lands. In modern times, the Kansas City Chiefs wear this symbol proudly as they defend their home field.

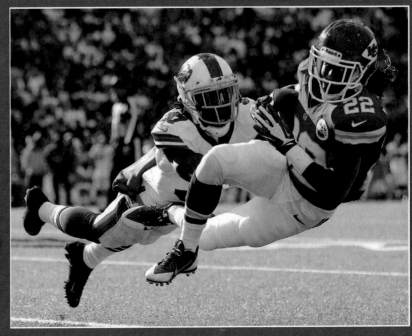

Late hits to the helmet after a play is stopped are cause for unsportsmanlike conduct and a 15-yard penalty.

The Coaches

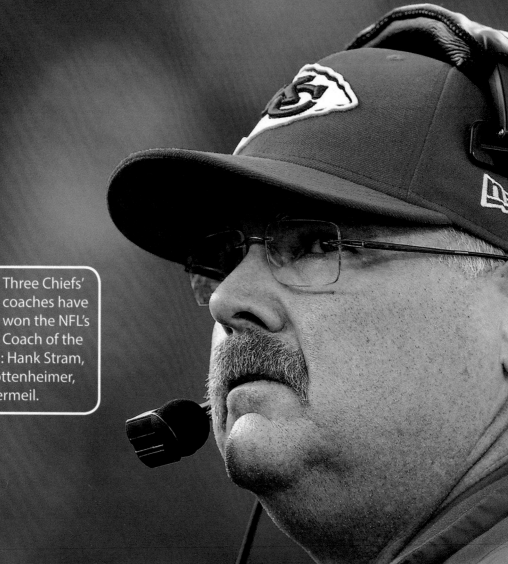

3 Three Chiefs' coaches have won the NFL's Coach of the Year Award: Hank Stram, Marty Schottenheimer, and Dick Vermeil.

Andy Reid's teams in Philadelphia and Kansas City have missed the playoffs just five times during his 15-year coaching career.

NFL Films asked Chiefs' coach Hank Stram to wear a microphone during Super Bowl IV. The footage revealed Stram to be a new breed of coach. He was smart, passionate, and extremely funny. Stram's humor kept things light on the Kansas City sideline. The Chiefs won the Super Bowl and had fun doing it.

HANK STRAM

The developer of the Tight **I formation** and the "two tight end" offenses, Hank Stram's strategic genius is still on display every Sunday when current NFL teams use his offensive schemes. Stram coached the Chiefs to three AFL Championships and one Super Bowl title, and the hall of fame coach did it without the aid of an offensive or defensive coordinator.

MARTY SCHOTTENHEIMER

As the head coach of the Kansas City Chiefs, Marty Schottenheimer brought intensity and focus to each game. He won a Chiefs' franchise-record 101 games while leading the Chiefs to three division titles and seven playoff appearances.

ANDY REID

Andy Reid left Philadelphia with the Eagles' franchise-record 130 wins. He led the team to four straight National Football Conference (NFC) Championship Games, one Super Bowl appearance, and was twice named Coach of the Year. In Reid's first year in Kansas City, he took a 2-14 squad and turned them into an 11-5 playoff team.

The Mascot

K.C. Wolf does not have much of a commute to work, as his den is located in the basement of Arrowhead Stadium.

The Chiefs official mascot is K.C. Wolf, a seven-foot, two-inch canine named for a famous group of rabid Chiefs fans called the "Wolfpack." They used to watch Chiefs' games from the temporary bleachers at Municipal Stadium. While he's a bit round around the middle, K.C. Wolf is a terrific athlete and showman. During games, he entertains fans with stunts, dances, and comedy routines. In 2006, in honor of his contribution to the Chiefs and their fans, K.C. Wolf became the first mascot ever to be inducted into the online-only Mascot Hall of Fame.

A horse named Warpaint is Kansas City's alternate mascot.

Entertaining fans alongside K.C. Wolf is a horse named Warpaint. A Kansas City Chiefs cheerleader rides Warpaint up and down the sidelines during home games.

K.C. Wolf enjoys wolf-themed culture. His favorite song is "Hungry Like the Wolf," and his favorite book is *Little Red Riding Hood*.

Legends of the Past

Many great players have suited up in the Chiefs red and gold. A few of them have become icons of the team and the city it represents.

Christian Okoye

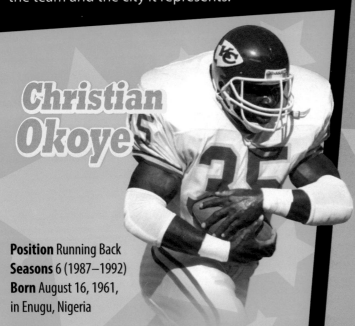

Position Running Back
Seasons 6 (1987–1992)
Born August 16, 1961, in Enugu, Nigeria

As a member of his college track and field team, Nigerian-born Christian Okoye won several medals in shot put, discuss, and hammer throw. When he joined the Azusa Pacific University's football team at the age of 23, he had never played a single football game, but at 6 feet, 1 inch tall and 260 pounds, Okoye was incredibly fast. This combination of speed and size caught the Chiefs' attention and they drafted him in 1987. In 1989, Okoye enjoyed his best season as a pro, leading the NFL with 1,480 rushing yards and earning the nickname "The Nigerian Nightmare." In six seasons, Okoye set a then-Chiefs' record for all-time rushing yards (4,897) and rushed for 40 touchdowns.

Derrick Thomas

In 1990, Derrick Thomas set a Chiefs' single season record with 20 **sacks**. This included an NFL-record seven sacks in a single game. That same year he created the Third and Long Foundation, a charity that helps to educate urban children.

In his 11-year career, Thomas set Chiefs' records for sacks (126.5), safeties (3), fumble recoveries (19), and forced fumbles (45). Between 1989 and 1997, Thomas appeared in nine straight Pro Bowls. Tragically, Thomas died from a car accident in 2000. He was only 33 years old.

Position Linebacker
Seasons 11 (1989–1999)
Born January 1, 1967, in Miami, Florida

Len Dawson

In 1962, the Dallas Texans traded Len Dawson from the Cleveland Browns and changed him from a reserve quarterback, who only played if the starting quarterback was injured or having an off day, into the most dominant passer in the AFL. In his first year in Dallas, Dawson led the AFL in touchdowns (29) and **passer rating** (98.3). He also led the Texans to an AFL Championship. The Texans moved to Kansas City in 1963 and changed their name to Chiefs, but a change in scenery did not affect Dawson's success. Between 1962 and 1969, Dawson made six AFL All-Star games, and quarterbacked the Chiefs' offense to three AFL titles and one Super Bowl title. Following the AFL-NFL merger, Dawson made one Pro Bowl in 1971 before retiring from football in 1975.

Position Quarterback
Seasons 19 (1957–1975)
Born June 20, 1935, in Alliance, Ohio

Tony Gonzalez

In 17 NFL seasons, Tony Gonzalez did not just set the record for most receptions by a tight end, he became the league's second all-time leading receiver behind Jerry Rice. One of the most durable players in NFL history, Gonzalez missed just one game due to injury in his career. He also had the surest pair of hands in the league. During his final 14 seasons, Gonzalez caught 1,145 passes and fumbled only once. In 12 years with the Chiefs, Gonzalez made 10 straight Pro Bowls, registered more than 1,000 receiving yards four times, and led the NFL in receptions (102) in 2004.

Position Tight End
Seasons 17 (1997–2013)
Born February 27, 1976, in Torrance, California

Stars of Today

Today's Chiefs team is made up of many young, talented players who have proven that they are among the best players in the league.

Eric Berry

A two-time All-American, Eric Berry received 22 awards during his three years with the Tennessee Volunteers. As a result, he entered his first year in the NFL with high expectations. Berry responded, starting all 16 games and becoming the first Chiefs rookie since Derrick Thomas to make the Pro Bowl. Berry missed the 2011 season with a knee injury but returned in 2012, earning another trip to the Pro Bowl. In 2013 he registered a career-best 3.5 sacks and returned two of his three interceptions for touchdowns.

Position Safety
Seasons 4 (2010–2013)
Born December 29, 1988, in Atlanta, Georgia

Alex Smith

In seven years with the San Francisco 49ers, Alex Smith steadily improved. Through the first nine games of the 2012 season, he was among the league leaders with a 104.3 passer rating. When an injury sidelined him, however, Smith lost his job to rookie Colin Kaepernick. In February of 2013, the Chiefs acquired Smith for a second round draft pick. In his first season in Kansas City, Smith passed for more than 3,000 yards and threw 23 touchdown passes against just seven interceptions. His steady play at quarterback was key in transforming the Chiefs from a last place team into a Super Bowl contender.

Position Quarterback
Seasons 8 (2005–2013)
Born May 7, 1984, in Bremerton, Washington

Jamaal Charles

In six seasons with the Chiefs, Jamaal Charles has become one of the best running backs in the NFL. A terrific runner and receiver, Charles led the NFL in rushing touchdowns (12) and receiving/rushing touchdowns (19) in 2013. His 1,980 **yards from scrimmage** earned him his third trip to the Pro Bowl in four years. An knee injury caused Charles to miss 14 games in 2011, but he has since regained the speed that made him a college track and field star. In 2014, barring injury, Charles could pass Priest Holmes to become the Chiefs' all-time leading rusher.

Position Running Back
Seasons 6 (2008–2013)
Born December 27, 1986, in Port Arthur, Texas

Tamba Hali

At the age of 10, Tamba Hali escaped with his father from war-torn Liberia on the east coast of Africa. They moved to Teaneck, New Jersey, where Hali vowed to develop into a professional football player so he could bring his mother to the United States. Entering the 2006 **NFL Draft**, Hali was considered a bit undersized to play defensive tackle in the NFL. However, noting his athletic ability and strength of character, the Chiefs selected him in the first round. In his rookie season, Hali led all NFL rookies with 8.5 sacks. He has since been named to two Pro Bowls.

Position Linebacker
Seasons 8 (2006–2013)
Born November 3, 1983, in Gbarnga, Liberia

All-Time Records

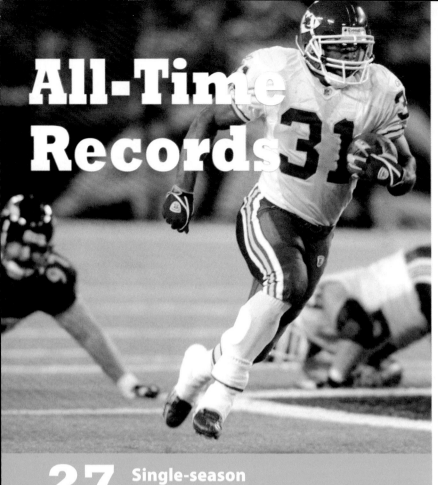

27 Single-season Rushing Touchdowns

In 2003, Priest Holmes set a then-NFL record with 27 rushing touchdowns.

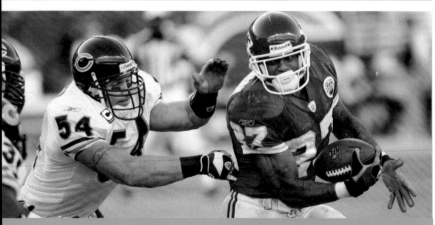

1,789 Single-season Rushing Yards

In 2006, Larry Johnson averaged 111.8 rushing yards per game on the way to setting the Chiefs' single-season rushing record.

10,940 Career Receiving Yards

Tight end Tony Gonzalez set the Chiefs' all-time receiving record during 12 brilliant seasons in Kansas City.

4,591

Single-season Passing Yards

In 2004, Trent Green threw for 27 touchdowns and a team-record 4,591 yards.

28,507 Career Passing Yards

Len Dawson set the Chiefs' record for all-time passing yards while leading the squad to three AFL Championships.

Timeline

Throughout the team's history, the Kansas City Chiefs have had many memorable events that have become defining moments for the team and its fans.

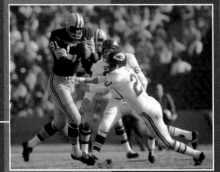

1966

Before the season, Chiefs' running back Mack Lee Hill dies during knee surgery. The team rallies to win 11 games. They then defeat the Buffalo Bills, 31-7, in the AFL Championship Game to win their first title since moving to Kansas City. In Super Bowl I, they lose to the Green Bay Packers. This is the first game to pit the AFL champion against the NFL champion.

1960

In the AFL's inaugural season, Lamar Hunt's Dallas Texans play in the Cotton Bowl in Dallas, Texas. Rookie head coach Hank Stram guides the Texans to an 8-6 record, but the Texans fail to make the playoffs.

On December 25, 1971, the Chiefs play their final game at Municipal Stadium.

| 1960 | 1965 | 1970 | 1975 | 1980 | 1985 |

1986

After missing the playoffs for 14-years, the Chiefs go 10-6 and make the playoffs for the first time since moving into Arrowhead Stadium in 1972. However, without any real offensive leaders, the Chiefs lose the wild card game to the New York Jets, 35-15.

1963

Lamar Hunt decides to move the Texans to Kansas City after 35,000 Kansas City football fans make payments on season tickets without even knowing which team they are paying to see. The Texans rename themselves the "Chiefs" and move into Municipal Stadium with Major League Baseball's Kansas City Athletics.

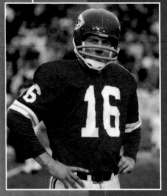

January 11, 1970

Despite being 13-point underdogs to the Minnesota Vikings, the Chiefs' defense dominates Super Bowl IV, allowing just 67 rushing yards and causing five turnovers. The Chiefs win their first Super Bowl title, and Len Dawson is named the game's **most valuable player (MVP)**.

CHIEFS

The Future
New arrivals Andy Reid and Alex Smith have found a home in Kansas City, and Chiefs fans could not be any happier. In joining a team with Pro Bowlers on both sides of the ball, Smith and Reid helped lead the Chiefs back to the playoffs. They showed everyone that the team's fast start to the 2013 season was no fluke.

1995
Marty Schottenheimer wins Coach of the Year in a season in which he guides the Chiefs to a franchise-record 13 wins. Pro Bowlers Neil Smith and Derrick Thomas combine for 20 sacks, but the Chiefs fall in the divisional round of the playoffs to the Indianapolis Colts, 10-7.

In 2010, the Chiefs win the AFC West, but are beaten by the Baltimore Ravens in the playoffs.

| 1990 | 1995 | 2000 | 2005 | 2010 | 2015 |

The Chiefs get their first playoff win at Arrowhead Stadium in 1991.

1990
Derrick Thomas sets an NFL record with seven sacks in a single game against the Seattle Seahawks. He finishes the season with an NFL-best 20 sacks. The Chiefs advance to the playoffs but give up 14 fourth-quarter points to the Miami Dolphins in a devastating 17-16 defeat.

2013
The Chiefs become the second team in NFL history to start a season 9-0 after finishing the previous season with the league's worst record. The defense is fantastic, and Alex Smith throws 23 touchdown passes to help out the offense. With a record of 11-5, Kansas City makes the playoffs.

W.ite a Biog.aphy

Life Story

A person's life story can be the subject of a book. This kind of book is called a biography. Biographies often describe the lives of people who have achieved great success. These people may be alive today, or they may have lived many years ago. Reading a biography can help you learn more about a great person.

Get the Facts

Use this book, and research in the library and on the Internet, to find out more about your favorite Chief. Learn as much about this player as you can. What position does he play? What are his statistics in important categories? Has he set any records? Also, be sure to write down key events in the person's life. What was his childhood like? What has he accomplished off the field? Is there anything else that makes this person special or unusual?

Use the Concept Web

A concept web is a useful research tool. Read the questions in the concept web on the following page. Answer the questions in your notebook. Your answers will help you write a biography.

Concept Web

□

Adulthood
- Where does this individual currently reside?
- Does he or she have a family?

□

Your Opinion
- What did you learn from the books you read in your research?
- Would you suggest these books to others?
- Was anything missing from these books?

□

Childhood
- Where and when was this person born?
- Describe his or her parents, siblings, and friends.
- Did this person grow up in unusual circumstances?

□

Accomplishments off the Field
- What is this person's life's work?
- Has he or she received awards or recognition for accomplishments?
- How have this person's accomplishments served others?

Write a Biography

□

Help and Obstacles
- Did this individual have a positive attitude?
- Did he or she receive help from others?
- Did this person have a mentor?
- Did this person face any hardships?
- If so, how were the hardships overcome?

□

Accomplishments on the Field
- What records does this person hold?
- What key games and plays have defined his or her career?
- What are his or her stats in categories important to his or her position?

□

Work and Preparation
- What was this person's education?
- What was his or her work experience?
- How does this person work; what is the process he or she uses?

Trivia Time

Take this quiz to test your knowledge of the Kansas City Chiefs.
The answers are printed upside-down under each question.

1 Who set the Chiefs' single-season rushing record in 2006 with 1,789 yards?

A. Larry Johnson

2 Which former coach of the Philadelphia Eagles guided the Chiefs to the 2013 playoffs?

A. Andy Reid

3 Which Kansas City Chiefs' mascot is ridden by a Chiefs cheerleader?

A. Warpaint

4 Who is the Chiefs all-time sacks leader?

A. Derrick Thomas

5 Who quarterbacked the Chiefs to three AFL Championships?

A. Len Dawson

6 Which NFL powerhouse did the Chiefs defeat to win Super Bowl IV?

A. Minnesota Vikings

7 Which former Los Angeles Raiders running back signed with the Chiefs in 1993?

A. Marcus Allen

8 Which Chiefs' linebacker escaped from a civil war in Liberia?

A. Tamba Hali

9 Which former San Francisco 49ers quarterback signed with the Chiefs in 2013?

A. Alex Smith

10 Who coached the Chiefs to their only Super Bowl title?

A. Hank Stram

Key Words

hall of fame: group of persons judged to be outstanding, as in a sport or profession

I formation: one of the most common offensive formations in American football. It draws its name from the vertical alignment of quarterback, fullback, and running back

inaugural: marking the beginning of an institution, activity, or period of office

logo: a symbol that stands for a team or organization

merger: a combination of two things, especially companies, into one

most valuable player (MVP): the player judged to be most valuable to his team's success

NFL Draft: an annual event where the NFL chooses college football players to be new team members

passer rating: a rating given to quarterbacks that tries to measure how well they perform on the field

postseason: a sporting event that takes place after the end of the regular season

Pro Bowlers: NFL players who take part in the annual all-star game that pits the best players in the National Football Conference (NFC) against the best players in the American Football Conference (AFC)

sacks: a sack occurs when the quarterback is tackled behind the line of scrimmage before he can throw a forward pass

Super Bowl: the NFL's annual championship game between the winning team from the NFC and the winning team from the AFC

yards from scrimmage: the total of rushing yards and receiving yards; scrimmage is the yard-line on the field from which the play starts

Index

Log on to www.av2books.com

AV² by Weigl brings you media enhanced books that support active learning. Go to www.av2books.com, and enter the special code found on page 2 of this book. You will gain access to enriched and enhanced content that supplements and complements this book. Content includes video, audio, weblinks, quizzes, a slide show, and activities.

AV² Online Navigation

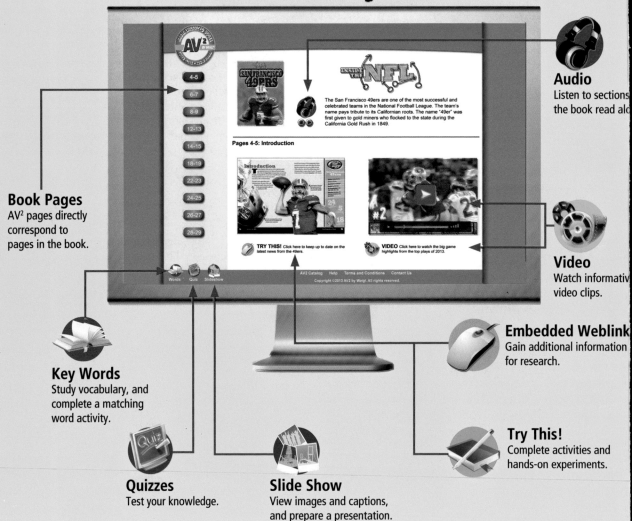

Book Pages
AV² pages directly correspond to pages in the book.

Audio
Listen to sections the book read alo

Video
Watch informativ video clips.

Embedded Weblink
Gain additional information for research.

Key Words
Study vocabulary, and complete a matching word activity.

Try This!
Complete activities and hands-on experiments.

Quizzes
Test your knowledge.

Slide Show
View images and captions, and prepare a presentation.

AV² was built to bridge the gap between print and digital. We encourage you to tell us what you like and what you want to see in the future.

Sign up to be an AV² Ambassador at www.av2books.com/ambassador.

Due to the dynamic nature of the Internet, some of the URLs and activities provided as part of AV² by Weigl may have changed or ceased to exist. AV² by Weigl accepts no responsibility for any such changes. All media enhanced books are regularly monitored to update addresses and sites in a timely manner. Contact AV² by Weigl at 1-866-649-3445 or av2books@weigl.com with any questions, comments, or feedback.